W9-BPR-150

An Educational Coloring Book
of
KACHINA DOLLS

EDITOR
Linda Spizzirri

ASST. EDITOR
Jacqueline Sontheimer

ILLUSTRATION
Peter M. Spizzirri

COVER ART
Peter M. Spizzirri

CONTENTS

An Educational Coloring Book of KACHINA DOLLS • Published by SPIZZIRRI PUBLISHING, INC., P.O. BOX 9397, RAPID CITY, SOUTH DAKOTA 57709. No part of this publication may be reproduced by any means without the express written consent of the publisher. All national and international rights reserved on the entire contents of this publication.
Printed in U.S.A.

WHAT IS A KACHINA DOLL?

Many of the Pueblo Indians have special ceremonies with masked men that they call "Kachinas". These Kachinas are the most important people in their ceremonies. The good Kachinas are similar to Christian saints and are supposed to be the spirits of very good men. However, not all Kachinas are representative of good spirits, some are bad spirits and demons.

For days before a Kachina ceremony, fathers, grandfathers and uncles are busy making dolls in the likeness of the Kachina dancers. These Kachina dolls are most important to the Hopi and the Zuni Indians, because they represent some of the supernatural beings that exist in many of the Pueblo ceremonies and dances.

To Hopi Indian children, the Kachinas are like Santa Claus, bringing gifts of Kachina dolls at certain seasons. On the day of the ceremony, each child of the village is given a doll made just for them by their relatives. The dolls are taken home by the children, and their parents hang the dolls on the walls or ceilings so they can always be seen by the children. This is the way the Hopi children learn to know all the different Kachinas and what they look like.

To the Hopi Indians, Kachina dolls are not idols to be worshiped or prayed to, but they are merely objects used to teach their children about good and evil.

HOW TO COLOR THE KACHINA DOLLS

The diagram below points out and labels the different parts of the Kachina dolls. The Kachinas have different kinds of masks, head pieces, different parts of clothing and are bare foot or are wearing either moccasins or boots. Not all of the things the Kachina dolls are wearing have to be specific colors. If there are no specific color instructions given, use any color you wish. These identifications will help you to do realistic colorings of the Kachina dolls.

If you find a term in the coloring instructions that you do not understand, please refer back to these diagrams for assistance.

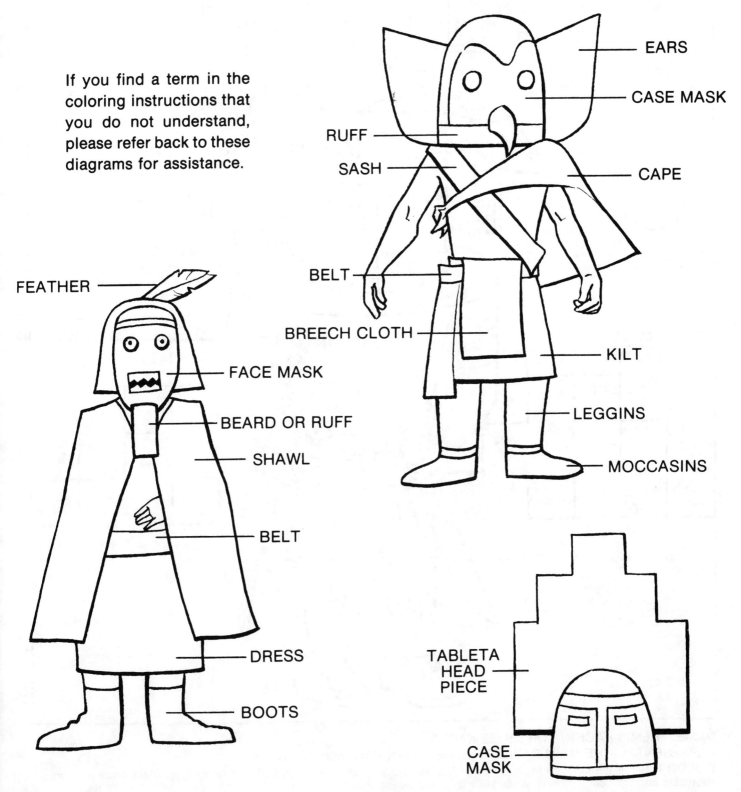

EARS

CASE MASK

RUFF

SASH

CAPE

FEATHER

FACE MASK

BEARD OR RUFF

SHAWL

BELT

DRESS

BOOTS

BELT

BREECH CLOTH

KILT

LEGGINS

MOCCASINS

TABLETA HEAD PIECE

CASE MASK

NAME: HEMIS KACHINA OR JEMEZ KACHINA
REPRESENTS: THE MAIN DANCER IN THE NIMAN KACHINA DANCE
COLOR IT: Case mask - half green, half pink. Head tableta - different colors. Green fir springs. Black body with green shoulders and light color moons. White kilt with green leaves. Red moccasins.

4

NAME: THE CROW MOTHER, ANGWUSNASOMTAQA OR TUMAS
REPRESENTS: KACHINA IN BEAN DANCE WHO SOME CALL "THE MOTHER OF ALL THE KACHINAS"
COLOR IT: Green mask with black crow wing ears. Black shape on face with white spots for eyes and mouth. Green woman's dress and ceremonial robe with green moccasins.

NAME: GREAT HORNED OWL KACHINA OR MONGWA
REPRESENTS: KACHINA DANCER WHO SPIES ON THE HANO CLOWNS
COLOR IT: White case mask and body paint; yellow eyes, ear wings and beak; red moccasins. Deer skin cape.

NAME: HILILI KACHINA
REPRESENTS: THE LEADING DANCER IN THE HILILI KACHINA DANCE
COLOR IT: Case mask is colored with white, blues and brown. Body is red with white designs; red leg decorations and moccasins. Wildcat skin collar.

7

NAME: SIO SALAKO OR ZUNI SALAKO
REPRESENTS: A 9 FOOT GIANT WHO APPEARS IN A SPECIAL ZUNI SALAKO DANCE
COLOR IT: Case mask is green with black band across eyes and on horns. Eagle feather robe with black trim. Red stripes on ceremonial shawl; green moccasins.

NAME: TURNED-DOWN BEAK OR TASAF (A NAVAJO KACHINA)
REPRESENTS: DANCER IN ALL REGULAR KACHINA DANCES
COLOR IT: Case mask - green; body - pink with yellow stripes; red mocassins; red hair on head and red tufts for ears.

9

NAME: NAVAHO KACHINA MAIDEN OR QOIA KACHIN-MANA
REPRESENTS: THE KACHINA MAIDEN WHO DANCES WITH THE QOIA KACHINA
COLOR IT: Green face mask with white eyes. Red and yellow stripes on cheeks. Clothing any color. White boots.

NAME: HANO CLOWN OR KOSHARE
REPRESENTS: THE KOSHARE WHO HAD SACRED POWERS AND APPEARED IN MANY DANCES
COLOR IT: White face and body; black stripes and feet; any color breech cloth.

11

NAME: SIP-IKNE OR ZUNI WARRIOR KACHINA
REPRESENTS: WARRIOR KACHINA WHO APPEARS IN THE BEAN DANCE AND REGULAR DANCES
COLOR IT: Mask any color; white eye mask; black body with yellow shoulders, stripes and forearms; white kilt with colored designs; bare feet and hands.

12

NAME: HUTUTU OR ZUNI RAIN PRIEST
REPRESENTS: KACHINA WHO APPEARS IN THE BEAN DANCE, MAKING A SOUND LIKE "HU—TU—TU"
COLOR IT: White case mask; body white with small black dots; clothing any color; fox skin over shoulder.

NAME: NATA-ASKA OR BLACK OGRE
REPRESENTS: KACHINA WHO ACCOMPANIES SOYOKO
COLOR IT: Black case mask; green crow foot on forehead; white eyes and teeth; red lips. White shirt; silver belt; red leggings and moccasins.

14

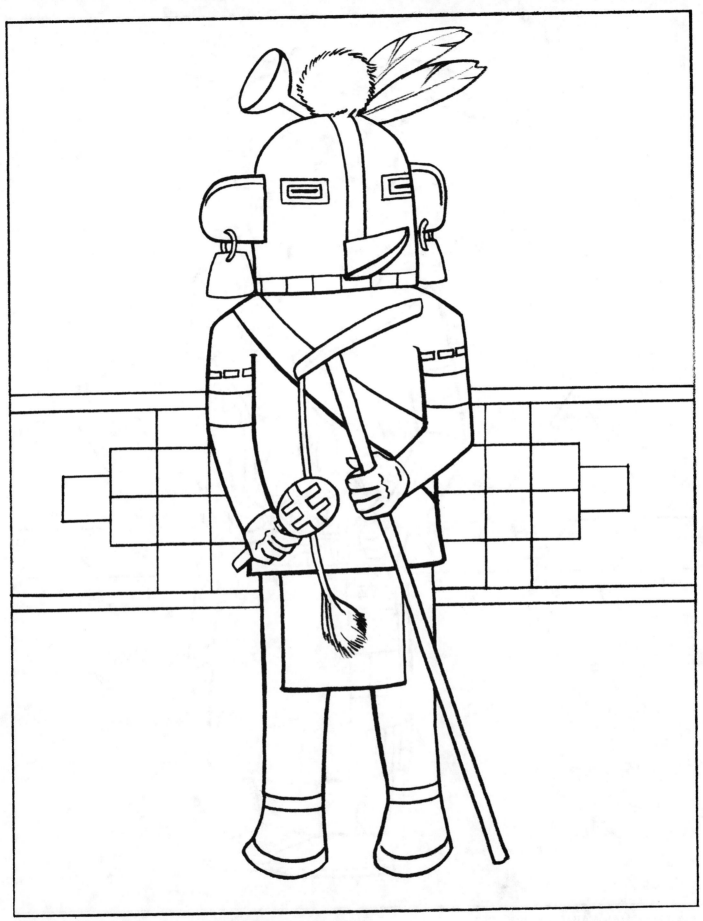

NAME: KOKO POLO OR TURNED-UP BEAK KACHINA
REPRESENTS: KACHINA WHO APPEARS IN MIXED KACHINA DANCES
COLOR IT: Green case mask; white eyes and stripe; shell earrings; white shirt with orange stitches and arm bands.
Breechcloth and moccasins any color.

15

NAME: CHAKWAINA-ZUNI KACHINA

REPRESENTS: KACHINA WHO APPEARS IN THE ZUNI PAMUYA DANCE

COLOR IT: Black face mask; black body with yellow shoulders and forearms; white eyes and mouth; red tongue; wooly lamb skin hair.

16

NAME: MOSAIRU KACHINA OR BUFFALO KACHINA
REPRESENTS: REGULAR KACHINA DANCER
COLOR IT: Green face mask; black nose shape; light color body painting; white kilt; red mocassins.

NAME: ANTELOPE KACHINA
REPRESENTS: KACHINA WHO APPEARS IN MIXED KACHINA DANCES
COLOR IT: White face mask with black designs; brown antelope horns; black decorations on kilt; yellow body designs and cane; green moccasins.

18

NAME: AVACHHOYA OR SPOTTED CORN KACHINA
REPRESENTS: KACHINA WHO APPEARS IN PAMUYA AND REGUALR KACHINA DANCES
COLOR IT: Case mask of many colors; pink body with white circles; red moccasins.

NAME: SNOW KACHINA MAIDEN
REPRESENTS: KACHINA APPEARS IN SNOW KACHINA DANCE AND THE NIMAN KACHINA DANCE
COLOR IT: White sack mask; white cotton hair; woman's dress any color; maiden's shawl any color; white boots.

20

NAME: POWAMUI KACHINA OR BEAN DANCE KACHINA
REPRESENTS: THE MOST IMPORTANT ACTORS IN THE BEAN DANCE
COLOR IT: Red face mask; black hair; carved multi-colored flowers in hair; white body; one shoulder decoration green and the other shoulder yellow; white kilt; red mocassins.

21

NAME: HOOTE OR AHOTE
REPRESENTS: KACHINA WHO APPEARS IN MIXED KACHINA DANCES
COLOR IT: Black case mask; yellow and red horns; yellow and red stripes on forehead; white moon and star on cheeks; red body with yellow forearms and shoulders; red moccasins.

NAME: HE-E-E
REPRESENTS: KACHINA WHO APPEARS IN ALL REGULAR KACHINA DANCES
COLOR IT: Black face mask; white eyes and teeth; red lips; white sash; dress and shawl are any color; red moccasins.

NAME: HEMIS KACHIN-MANA OR KACHINA MAIDEN
REPRESENTS: KACHINA WHO APPEARS WITH THE HEMIS KACHINA AND MANY OTHER KACHINAS
COLOR IT: Yellow mask with red hair for maiden whorls; any color on shawl and dress; white boots.

NAME: KONIN KACHINA OR SUPAI KACHINA
REPRESENTS: KACHINA WHO APPEARS IN REGULAR KACHINA DANCES
COLOR IT: White face mask; different color squares on the face; red sash and moccasins. Fox skin kilt.

NAME: HU KACHINA OR TONGWUP WHIPPER KACHINA
REPRESENTS: KACHINA WHO APPEARS IN THE BEAN DANCE WITH CROW MOTHER AND THE WHIP CHILDREN.
COLOR IT: Black case mask; white spots on cheeks; white turkey track on forehead; red moccasins. Fox skin ruff.

NAME: YUCCA KACHINA OR YUCCA SKIRT MAN
REPRESENTS: KACHINA WHO DANCES TO BRING COLD WEATHER
COLOR IT: Green case mask; white cheek circles; green douglas fir ruff; silver belt circles; tan color yucca leaf skirt; red moccasins.

NAME: MASTOF KACHINA
REPRESENTS: KACHINA WHO APPEARS IN THE SOLSTICE CEREMONY
COLOR IT: Black case mask; white eyes, mouth and dots; black body with white hand designs; red mocassins.

NAME: POLIK MANA OR BUTTERFLY KACHINA MAIDEN
REPRESENTS: KACHINA BUTTERFLY DANCER
COLOR IT: White face mask tableta; red stripes on cheeks; chin has multi-color lines; white costume with decorations in many different colors; bare feet are painted yellow.

29

NAME: NAKIACHOP OR SILENT KACHINA
REPRESENTS: KACHINA WHO APPEARS IN WATER SERPENT CEREMONY AND THE BEAN DANCE
COLOR IT: Green case mask; black eyes and nose; black and white squares on forehead and mouth; white shawl decorated in many colors.

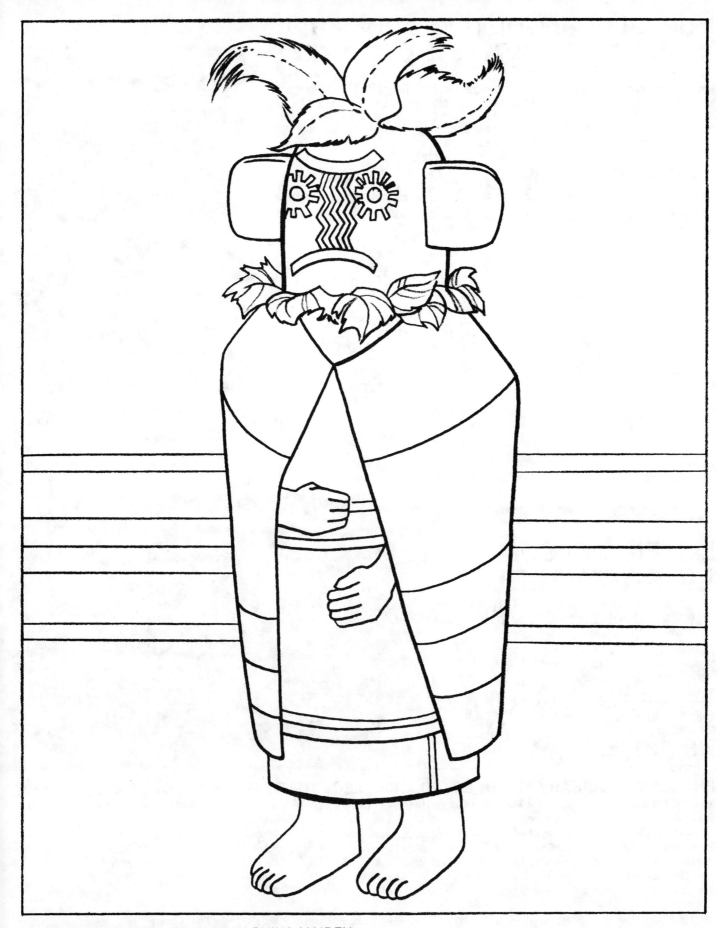

NAME: HOHO MANA OR ZUNI KACHINA MAIDEN
REPRESENTS: KACHINA WHO APPEARS WITH THE HEMIS KACHINA
COLOR IT: Black case mask; white blossom eyes and white zigzag nose marks; clothing of any colors.

Educational Coloring Books and
STORY CASSETTES

The only non-fiction coloring book/cassette packages available! The cassettes are not read-alongs. Rather, the educational factual information in the coloring book is utilized and enhanced to create exciting stories. Sound, music, and professional narration stimulate interest and promote reading. Children can color and listen, color alone, or simply listen to the cassette. We are proud to offer these quality products at a reasonable price.

DISPLAY RACKS AVAILABLE. INDIVIDUALLY PACKAGED.

YOUR CHOICE OF 48 TITLES

"ISBN (INTERNATIONAL STANDARD BOOK NUMBER) PREFIX ON ALL BOOKS AND CASSETTES: 0-86545-

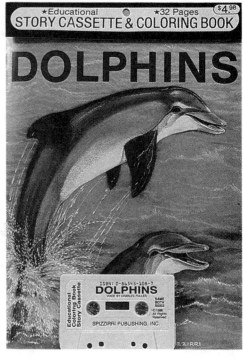

No. 082-X DINOSAURS	No. 161-3 DOGS
No. 083-8 Prehistoric SEA LIFE	No. 162-1 HORSES
No. 084-6 Prehistoric BIRDS	No. 159-1 BIRDS
No. 085-4 CAVE MAN	No. 147-8 PENGUINS
No. 086-2 Prehistoric FISH	No. 098-6 STATE BIRDS
No. 087-0 Prehistoric MAMMALS	No. 163-X STATE FLOWERS
No. 097-8 Count/Color DINOSAURS	No. 100-1 MAMMALS
No. 089-7 PLAINS INDIANS	No. 101-X REPTILES
No. 090-0 NORTHEAST INDIANS	No. 158-3 POISONOUS SNAKES
No. 091-9 NORTHWEST INDIANS	No. 102-8 CATS OF THE WILD
NO. 092-7 SOUTHEAST INDIANS	No. 103-6 ENDANGERED SPECIES
No. 093-5 SOUTHWEST INDIANS	No. 157-5 PRIMATES
No. 094-3 CALIFORNIA INDIANS	No. 104-4 ANIMAL GIANTS
No. 153-2 ESKIMOS	No. 148-6 ATLANTIC FISH
No. 152-4 COWBOYS	No. 149-4 PACIFIC FISH
No. 150-8 COLONIES	No. 105-2 SHARKS
No. 151-6 PIONEERS	No. 106-0 WHALES
No. 154-0 FARM ANIMALS	No. 107-9 DEEP-SEA FISH
No. 095-1 DOLLS	No. 108-7 DOLPHINS
No. 096-X ANIMAL ALPHABET	No. 109-5 AIRCRAFT
No. 160-5 CATS	No. 110-9 SPACE CRAFT

No. 111-7 SPACE EXPLORERS	
No. 112-5 PLANETS	
No. 113-3 COMETS	
No. 114-1 ROCKETS	
No. 155-9 TRANSPORTATION	
No. 156-7 SHIPS	

ALL BOOK CASSETTE PACKAGES $4.98 EACH

LISTEN AND COLOR
LIBRARY ALBUMS

6 Educational Coloring Books
Book/Story Cassettes
In a plastic storage case

We have gathered cassettes and books of related subject matter into individual library albums. Each album will provide a new, in-depth, and lasting learning experience. They are presented in a beautiful binder that will store and protect your collection for years.
We also invite you to pick 6 titles of your chosing and create your own CUSTOM ALBUM.

LIBRARY ALBUMS $34.95 EACH

CHOOSE ANY LIBRARY ALBUM LISTED, OR SELECT TITLES FOR YOUR CUSTOM ALBUM

No. 088-9 Prehistoric Life
Dinosaurs
Prehistoric Sea Life
Prehistoric Fish
Prehistoric Birds
Prehistoric Mammals
Cave Man

No. 116-8 American Indian
Plains Indians
Northeast Indians
Northwest Indians
Southeast Indians
Southwest Indians
California Indians

No. 164-8 Oceans & Seas
Atlantic Fish
Pacific Fish
Sharks
Whales
Deep-Sea Fish
Dolphins

No. 117-6 Air & Space
Aircraft
Space Craft
Space Explorers
Planets
Comets
Rockets

No. 165-6 Americana
Colonies
Cowboys
Pioneers
State Flowers
State Birds
Endangered Species

No. 166-4 Animal Libr #1
Poisonous Snakes
Reptiles
Animal Giants
Mammals
Cats of the Wild
Primates

No. 167-2 Animal Libr. #2
Prehistoric Mammals
Birds
Farm Animals
Endangered Species
Animal Alphabet
State Birds

No. 168-0 Young Students
Animal Alphabet
Counting & Coloring Dinosaurs
Dolls
Dogs
Cats
Horses

No. 170-2 New Titles Library
Eskimos
State Flowers
Penguins
Atlantic Fish
Pacific Fish
Farm Animals

No. 169-9 Custom Library
WE INVITE YOU TO PICK 6 TITLES OF YOUR CHOSING AND CREATE YOUR OWN CUSTOM LIBRARY.